What's the Issue?

WHAT ARE POLITICAL CAMPAIGNS?

By Judy Thorpe

KidHaven
PUBLISHING

Published in 2022 by
KidHaven Publishing, an Imprint of Greenhaven Publishing, LLC
353 3rd Avenue
Suite 255
New York, NY 10010

Designer: Deanna Paternostro
Editor: Jennifer Lombardo

Photo credits: Cover (top) Niyazz/Shutterstock.com; cover (bottom) Hero Images/Hero Images/ Getty Images; p. 5 Everett - Art/Shutterstock.com; p. 7 chrisdorney/Shutterstock.com; p. 9 Rick Gershon/Getty Images; p. 11 (main) Adam Glanzman/Bloomberg via Getty Images; p. 11 (inset) Joseph Prezioso/AFP via Getty Images; p. 13 (top) Drew Angerer/Getty Images; p. 13 (bottom) David Garcia/Shutterstock.com; p. 15 (top, bottom) Darren McCollester/Getty Images; p. 19 (main) Ink Drop/Shutterstock.com; p. 19 (inset) ID1974/Shutterstock.com; p. 21 Mikado767/ Shutterstock.com.

Cataloging-in-Publication Data

Names: Thorpe, Judy.
Title: What are political campaigns? / Judy Thorpe.
Description: New York : KidHaven Publishing, 2022. | Series: What's the issue? | Includes glossary and index.
Identifiers: ISBN 9781534534605 (pbk.) | ISBN 9781534534629 (library bound) | ISBN 9781534534612 (6 pack) | ISBN 9781534534636 (ebook)
Subjects: LCSH: Political campaigns–United States–Juvenile literature. | Campaign management–United States–Juvenile literature.
Classification: LCC JK2281.T467 2022 | DDC 324.70973—dc23

Printed in the United States of America

Some of the images in this book illustrate individuals who are models. The depictions do not imply actual situations or events.

CPSIA compliance information: Batch #CS22KH: For further information contact Greenhaven Publishing LLC, New York, New York at 1-844-317-7404.

Please visit our website, www.greenhavenpublishing.com. For a free color catalog of all our high-quality books, call toll free 1-844-317-7404 or fax 1-844-317-7405.

Find us on

CONTENTS

What It Means to Campaign

In a democracy, someone can only hold certain leadership positions if the people of the country vote for them. In the United States, the ones that often get the most attention are the president, vice president, and members of Congress. However, there are also a lot of other government leaders, including leaders of a state, city, or county.

A political campaign is a way for a **candidate** to try to get people to vote for them. A campaign tells people who the candidate is, what they'll do if they're elected, and why they're a better choice than the other candidates.

Facing the Facts

There are more than 500,000 elected officials in the United States!

George Washington was the only U.S. president who didn't have to campaign to get people to vote for him.

Political Parties

A political party is a group of people who have the same ideas about what's best for a country. The United States has had political parties since it was created, but they've changed over the years. Today, the two biggest parties are the Democratic Party and the Republican Party.

A candidate running for a position in the government is almost always part of a political party. The party helps the candidate raise money for their campaign. People often support a certain party and vote for that party's candidate, so it's generally easier for someone to get elected if they're part of a well-known party.

Facing the Facts

Political parties have a lot of nicknames. Democrats are often called the "left." Republicans are often called the "right." Sometimes the Republican Party is also called the Grand Old Party (GOP).

Animals are used to represent, or stand for, the two main U.S. political parties. The animal that represents the Democratic Party is a donkey. The animal that represents the Republican Party is an elephant.

Getting Help

It takes a lot of work to run a campaign. A candidate can't do it alone! Many people work for their favorite candidate without being paid, just because they want to help the person win. These people are called volunteers. People who get paid to work on a campaign are called staff.

Every campaign needs a campaign manager to lead it and make most of the important decisions. It also needs a treasurer, or someone to keep track of how much money is being raised and spent. Another job is communications director. This person talks to the news and sets up **interviews** for the candidate.

Facing the Facts

Each campaign has a headquarters, or main office. Bigger campaigns often also have smaller offices in several states.

Campaign volunteers spend a lot of time making phone calls to ask people to vote for a candidate. Shown here are volunteers working on Barack Obama's campaign in 2007. Their work paid off—Obama was elected president the next year!

Making Promises

One of the biggest parts of a campaign is the promises a candidate makes to voters about the causes they'll support. Generally, these are the same causes their party supports. The party **nominates** a candidate that agrees with them.

It's important for voters to pay attention to more than just what a candidate promises. They also need to understand how the candidate plans to keep those promises. For example, if a candidate promises to lower taxes but doesn't say how they're going to do that, it's a sign that they might not have a good plan.

Facing the Facts

A slogan is a short **phrase** that helps people remember a candidate. In 2008, Barack Obama's slogan was "Change We Can Believe In." In 2016, Donald Trump's slogan was "Make America Great Again."

During a campaign, candidates **debate** each other to try to show that their ideas are the best, and they put their campaign slogan on things such as signs, pins, and hats.

Looking Good

Most people care as much about a candidate's style as they do about their plans. Part of this style is how the person looks. Someone who supports a candidate will often show photos of them looking **dignified**. Someone who opposes a candidate is more likely to show them looking silly or mean.

Style is also about how a candidate acts. Some people want to vote for a person who seems fun and nice. Other people think this means the candidate isn't **serious** enough about the job. They might want to vote for someone who seems more **aggressive**.

Facing the Facts

In 1960, John F. Kennedy and Richard Nixon **participated** in the first presidential debate shown on television. Many people believe Nixon lost the election because voters thought Kennedy looked better in the debate.

President Donald Trump

A candidate's gender can unfairly play a part in the way a voter thinks of them. Some people think a woman who looks angry is too aggressive to be a good leader. The same people might think a man who looks angry is showing that he's a strong leader.

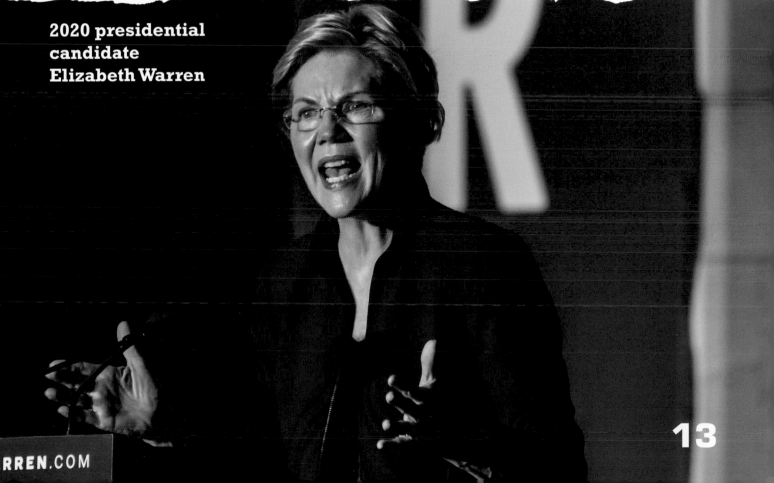

2020 presidential candidate Elizabeth Warren

13

Using Ads

To let voters know about their campaign, candidates put advertisements, or ads, on the internet, television, radio—almost anywhere! There are two general kinds of ads: positive and negative. A positive ad tells someone good things about a candidate and their plans. A negative ad tells people bad things about a candidate's **opponent**.

There are a lot of rules about what can and can't be said in a campaign ad. One of the rules is that the ad has to say who's paying for it. Another is that, if a radio or TV ad comes right from the candidate, they have to say out loud that they agree with the ad's message.

Facing the Facts

Dwight D. Eisenhower was the first U.S. presidential candidate to use television to advertise his campaign.

Shown here are two billboard ads that talk about the same candidate. The one on the bottom is a positive ad from Donald Trump's campaign. The one on the top is a negative ad Ted Cruz used when he ran against Trump in 2016.

Raising Money

Candidates need a lot of money to run a campaign. Aside from ads, they have to pay for things such as traveling to different states so they can talk to voters. The act of raising and spending money on a campaign is called campaign finance, and there are a lot of laws about it.

Many people say campaign finance laws need to be **reformed**. There are limits on how much money people can give to a candidate, but it's easy to get around those limits. Often, when a person or group gives a lot of money to a candidate, they expect the candidate to use their power to help them.

Facing the Facts

By law, a candidate can only spend $50,000 of their own money on their campaign. The rest has to come from donations.

Total Federal Election Spending

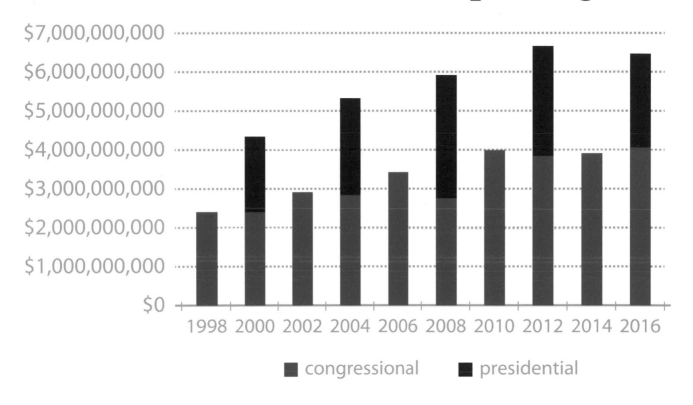

Shown here is a graph of the amount of money federal, or national, candidates have spent on their campaigns. The more they spend, the more money candidates need people to give them.

Fake News

After the 2016 U.S. presidential election, people started to realize that fake news on **social media** was a big problem. People would share things about candidates that weren't true. Many people who saw these fake news stories believed them and shared them with more people.

Most people think fake news will keep being a problem in elections from now on. However, not all news is fake news. Sometimes people say "fake news" when they see something they don't agree with. That's not the same thing! This can be confusing. It's important for people to do their own **research** instead of believing everything they read or hear.

Facing the Facts 🔍

In 2019, it was proven that Russians had posted fake news on social media to get people to vote for Donald Trump in the 2016 U.S. presidential election.

When people stop trusting the real news, it's easier for people to spread fake news. Many people are worried that Russians will keep spreading fake news.

Russian President Vladimir Putin

Taking a Stand

An important thing to remember about political campaigns is that they're all about trying to influence, or have an effect on, voters' opinions. Each campaign tries to get people to like one candidate better than all the others. Voters need to think carefully about what a campaign is telling them and do research to find out whether everything that's being said is true.

In the United States, you can't vote until you're 18, but there are lots of things you can do before then to get more involved with this issue. Everyone can make their voice heard, no matter how young they are!

Facing the Facts 🔍

In 1971, the voting age in the United States was lowered from 21 to 18.

WHAT CAN YOU DO?

Talk to the voters in your family about candidates and their campaigns.

Point out fake news when you see it.

Volunteer with an organization that helps people register, or sign up, to vote.

Volunteer to help with or raise money for your favorite candidate's campaign.

Research candidates' promises and the things they say in their campaign ads.

Vote when you turn 18.

Ask your teacher to set aside class time for everyone to talk about elections.

You can make a difference in an election long before you can vote!

GLOSSARY

aggressive: Seeming angry or ready to attack.

candidate: A person who runs in an election.

debate: An argument or discussion about an issue, generally between two sides. Also, to take part in such an argument or discussion.

dignified: Serious and somewhat formal.

interview: A meeting at which someone gets information from a person.

nominate: To formally choose someone as a candidate for a job or office.

opponent: A person or group that is facing another in a contest.

participate: To take part in.

phrase: A short expression that is commonly used.

reform: To change something in a way that makes it better.

research: Careful study that is done to find new knowledge about something.

serious: Giving a lot of thought or attention to something.

social media: A collection of websites and applications, or apps, that allow users to interact with each other and create online communities.

FOR MORE INFORMATION

WEBSITES

BrainPOP: Voting

www.brainpop.com/socialstudies/usgovernment/voting

Through videos, quizzes, games, and more, this interactive website teaches users all about voting, as well as what it takes to run a successful campaign.

Presidential Election Process

www.usa.gov/election

This government website explains how the presidential election process works.

BOOKS

Baicker, Karen. *The Election Activity Book.* New York, NY: Scholastic, 2016.

McPherson, Stephanie Sammartino. *Political Parties: From Nominations to Victory Celebrations.* Minneapolis, MN: Lerner Publications, 2016.

Weiss, Nancy E. *Asking Questions About Political Campaigns.* Ann Arbor, MI: Cherry Lake Publishing, 2016.

Publisher's note to educators and parents: Our editors have carefully reviewed these websites to ensure that they are suitable for students. Many websites change frequently, however, and we cannot guarantee that a site's future contents will continue to meet our high standards of quality and educational value. Be advised that students should be closely supervised whenever they access the Internet.

INDEX